THE GLORY OF GREECE

BETH ZEMBLE AND JOHN HOLDREN

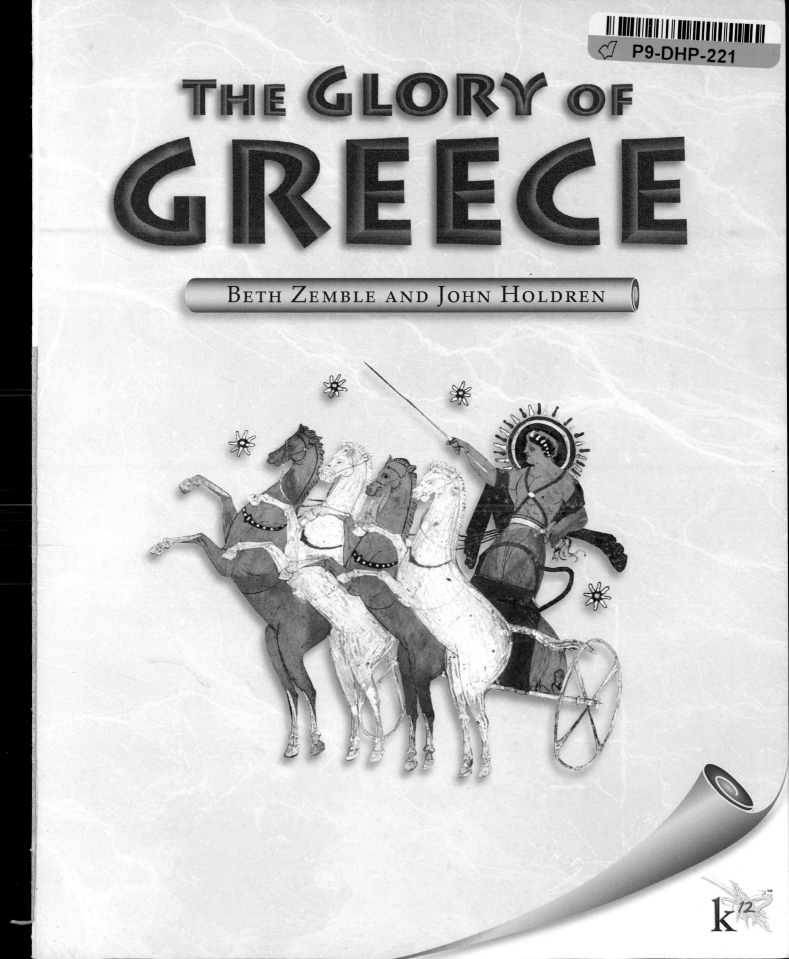

K12

Cover and Title Page Images

Front cover: The rocky hill called the Acropolis rises hundreds of feet above the city of Athens in Greece. On this hill, the most important site in the city in ancient times, sits the grand temple called the Parthenon.

Title page: Helios, the god of the sun in Greek mythology, drives his blazing chariot across the sky.

Back cover: The rocky land of Greece meets the waters of the Mediterranean Sea. The figures of three runners are from an ancient Greek vase, given as a prize to the winner of a race.

Staff for This Book

Bud Knecht *Project Manager*
Jeff Burridge *Editor*
Suzanne Montazer *Art Director*
Jayoung Cho *Designer*

Charlotte Fullerton *Illustrations Editor*
Betsy Woodman *Research Editor*
Martin Walz *Map Editor*
Lisa Dimaio Iekel *Production Manager*

About K12 Inc.

Founded in 1999, K12 Inc. is an elementary and secondary school service combining rich academic content with powerful technology. K¹² serves students in a variety of education settings, both public and private, including school classrooms, virtual charter schools, home schools, and tutoring centers. K¹² currently provides comprehensive curricular offerings in the following subjects: Language Arts/English, History, Math, Science, Visual Arts, and Music. The K¹² curriculum blends high quality offline materials with innovative online resources, including interactive lessons, teacher guides, and tools for planning and assessment. For more information, call 1-888-YOUR K12 or visit www.K12.com.

Library of Congress Cataloging-in-Publication Data

Zemble, Beth, 1968-
    The glory of Greece / by Beth Zemble and John Holdren.
        p. cm.
    Includes index.
    ISBN-13: 978-1-931728-81-2
    ISBN-10: 1-931728-81-X
    1. Greece--Civilization--To 146 B.C.--Juvenile literature. I. Holdren, John, 1954- II. Title.
    DF77.Z45 2006
    938--dc22

                                                            2006002418

Printed by Worzalla, Stevens Point, WI, USA, July 2018

CONTENTS

WHY STUDY ANCIENT GREECE?

Have you ever read stories about the powerful hero called Hercules? Or about a flying horse called Pegasus?

Have you ever seen the Olympic Games? Athletes try to see who can run the fastest, jump the highest, or lift the most weight.

Do you know what democracy is? It is a kind of government in which the people rule.

Fantastic stories, the Olympic Games, the idea of democracy—all of these are still with us today. And they all came to us from the land called Greece.

Look in the Glossary at the back of this book for the meanings of words in **bold** type.

Long ago, the Greek people built a great **civilization**. The Greeks made important discoveries in math, science, and medicine. They built beautiful buildings. They wrote exciting plays. They made lifelike statues. They thought of new and great ideas.

The ancient Greeks began to build their civilization in the eighth **century** B.C. Greek civilization was at its strongest for about four centuries. That is a long time—about 400 years. The United States is not yet 250 years old.

Let's find out why the ancient Greeks are still important to us today. Let's go back to the time when ancient Greece was in its glory.

WHAT DO B.C. AND A.D. MEAN?

Greece was in its glory in the fifth and fourth centuries B.C. What does B.C. mean?

The letters B.C. stand for *before Christ*. So, Greek civilization was thriving about 400 years before Jesus Christ was born.

For the years after the birth of Christ, we use the letters A.D. Those letters stand for the Latin words *anno Domini*, which mean "in the year of our Lord." In the year A.D. 1969, astronauts first walked on the moon.

Notice that you write A.D. *before* a number and B.C. *after* a number. Think about the year you were born. How you would write the year you were born?

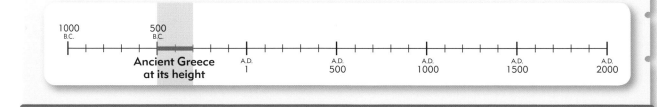

1000 B.C.   500 B.C.   Ancient Greece at its height   A.D. 1   A.D. 500   A.D. 1000   A.D. 1500   A.D. 2000

THE LAND AND SEAS

What kind of land was ancient Greece? How did the land affect people's lives?

The rocky soil of Greece makes it hard to grow crops. Only one-fourth of the land is good for farming.

ANCIENT GREECE

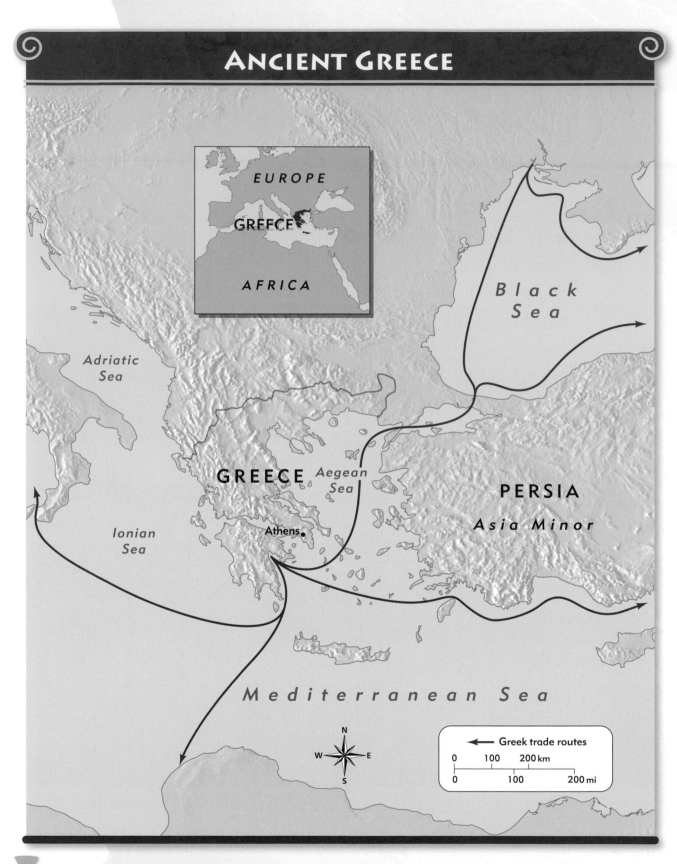

EUROPE

GREECE

AFRICA

Adriatic
Sea

Black
Sea

GREECE

Aegean
Sea

PERSIA

Asia Minor

Ionian
Sea

Athens

Mediterranean Sea

N
W E
S

Greek trade routes

0	100	200 km
0	100	200 mi

A Hard Land to Farm

In ancient Greece, it was hard to grow crops because of the long, dry summers and cold winters. Also, the land of Greece is mostly big, stony mountains. The hilly, rocky land made it hard to find good places for farming.

What did the Greeks grow on this rocky land? They grew grains, such as barley. They also grew grapes. From the grapes the Greeks made wine.

Olives were another main crop for Greek farmers. Olive trees grow well on the rocky Greek hillsides.

The Greeks thought the olive tree stood for strength and peace. Maybe that is because it could grow in hard places and survive in harsh conditions.

The Greeks raised sheep and goats. These animals gave them meat to eat and wool to make warm blankets for the winter.

Groves of olive trees thrive on the hillsides of Greece.

Many Uses for Olives

The Greeks found many uses for olives. Of course they ate olives. But they also crushed olives to make olive oil.

They used olive oil for cooking. They used it in oil lamps. They rubbed it on their skin. They sometimes used the oil as a kind of medicine. Athletes used to rub it all over their bodies before competing. A Greek poet called olive oil "liquid gold."

From the leafy branches of the olive tree, the Greeks wove crowns. They placed these crowns on the heads of those who won in sporting events.

Olives ripen on a branch.

People of the Sea

Some Greeks did not stay near the mountains and rivers. Instead, they followed the rivers to the coast and lived by the sea. So many people settled by the sea that one ancient Greek writer said they were like "frogs around a pond."

Look at the map on page 2. You will see that Greece is a **peninsula**. There is water on almost every side of Greece.

On one side is the Ionian Sea. On another side is the Aegean Sea. And most important of all is the Mediterranean Sea. Find these seas on the map.

These bodies of water shaped the lives of many people in ancient Greece. Some were fishermen. Some built ships to sail on the seas. Some were sailors and sea captains to sail the ships.

Merchants traveled in ships to nearby islands or faraway places to buy and sell their goods. Sometimes soldiers would sail with them to keep them safe.

There is water on three sides of Greece. Here you see the vivid blue waters of the Mediterranean Sea.

Let's Say It!
- Ionian (iy-OH-nee-uhn)
- Aegean (ih-JEE-uhn)
- Mediterranean (meh-duh-tuh-RAY-nee-uhn)

CHAPTER 2

MANY GODS AND GODDESSES

Where does lightning come from? Why do people fall in love? Why do countries fight wars?

The ancient Greeks answered these and many other questions by saying, "It is the will of the gods."

The ancient Greeks visited this shrine to the god Apollo to make offerings or to seek help and advice.

Long ago the Greeks worshipped many different gods and goddesses. They believed these gods and goddesses made things happen on Earth.

The Greeks believed that their gods and goddesses were in some ways like people. They had to eat and sleep. They could feel happy or sad. Sometimes they got angry. They argued and played tricks on each other. They could be mean one day and kind the next.

But there was one big difference between people and the gods. The Greeks believed their gods were immortal. That means they would live forever.

Zeus, the king of the gods, stands by an eagle, a symbol of his power.

GREEK GODS AND GODDESSES

Here are some of the main gods and goddesses that the people of ancient Greece worshipped.

- Zeus (zoos)—king of the gods
- Hera (HAIR-uh)—wife of Zeus, queen of the gods
- Athena (uh-THEE-nuh)—goddess of wisdom
- Aphrodite (a-fruh-DIY-tee)—goddess of love and beauty
- Eros (EHR-ohs)—the god of love and son of Aphrodite; later known as Cupid
- Ares (AIR-eez)—god of war
- Artemis (AHR-tuh-mus)—goddess of wildlife, the moon, and hunting
- Demeter (dih-MEE-tur)—goddess of grain and growing things
- Hephaestus (hih-FES-tus)—god of fire and the forge
- Hermes (HUR-meez)—the messenger god
- Apollo (uh-PAH-loh)—god of light, music, law, and reason
- Poseidon (puh-SIY-dn)—god of the sea
- Hades (HAY-deez)—god of the underworld
- Dionysus (diy-uh-NIY-sus)—god of wine
- Hestia (HES-tee-uh)—goddess of the hearth

Athena

Aphrodite

Apollo

This vase shows people making offerings to the god Apollo, who stands at far right, looking on.

The Greeks built temples and shrines to honor their gods. There they made offerings to the gods. Sometimes they left gifts of fruits and grains. Sometimes they sacrificed animals, such as sheep or goats.

The Greeks believed it was important to keep the gods happy. If the gods were unhappy, the people would suffer. If the gods were happy, all would go well.

TWO BIG WORDS

The ancient Greeks were *polytheists*. That means they believed in more than one god. People who believe in one God are called *monotheists*. *Poly* means "many." *Mono* means "one."

Let's Say It!

- polytheists (PAH-lee-THEE-ists)
- monotheists (MAH-nuh-THEE-ists)

Myths: Stories of the Gods

How do we know so much about the Greek gods? We know about them because the Greeks told many stories of the gods. We call these stories **myths**.

In these myths, the ancient Greeks explained things that people didn't understand. For example, why do

Artemis—the goddess of wildlife, the moon, and hunting—reaches for an arrow.

storms rage at sea? (Because the sea god, Poseidon, is angry.) Or why are there seasons? (For the answer, you will need to read the myth of Demeter and Persephone.)

Today we know the real reasons why storms happen and why seasons change. But we still read the old myths because they are such wonderful stories.

MYTHICAL CREATURES

In Greek myths, you will meet some amazing creatures. Some are beautiful, like the winged horse, Pegasus. Others are terrible monsters. The Minotaur was half-man and half-bull. The Gorgons looked like women with snakes instead of hair on their heads. Anyone who looked at the Gorgons was turned to stone!

The winged horse, Pegasus

Let's Say It!
• Persephone (pur-SEH-fuh-nee)
• Minotaur (MIH-nuh-tor)

The Judgment of Paris

Here is a myth that the Greeks told to explain the beginnings of a war between the Greeks and the Trojans, the people of the city of Troy.

At a fine palace in ancient Greece, many people gathered to celebrate a wedding. All the princes and princesses of that part of Greece were there. And all the gods and goddesses had been invited to attend.

Well, almost all—one goddess had not been invited. Her name was Eris. She was not invited because she liked to cause trouble.

As the winged god of love looks on, the bride and groom (at left) welcome the goddesses (at right) to their wedding.

As Eris looked down from Mount Olympus, she saw everyone having fun at the wedding feast. She felt sorry for herself. Then she got angry. She decided to make some mischief.

She made a golden apple. It shone with such beauty that it made the sun look dim.

Around the top of the apple, Eris wrote the words, "To the Fairest." She knew those words would cause trouble!

Eris waited until she saw Hera, the queen of the gods, chatting with two other goddesses, Athena and Aphrodite. Then she tossed the golden apple among them. "Now let's see what happens," she grinned.

Hera, queen of the gods, picked up the apple. She read the words on it—"To the Fairest." Then she said, "Why, this must be for me. No other goddess is as graceful as I am."

"My dear Hera," said Aphrodite. "The apple must be for me. I am the fairest. After all, I am the most beautiful goddess of all."

• Eris (EE-ris)

"Oh, no," said Athena, the goddess of wisdom. "The golden apple is for me. I am the fairest because I make the wisest decisions."

The three goddesses started to argue about who was the fairest. Then Hera said, "Wait! Let us ask my husband to say which of us deserves the apple. After all, he is the king of the gods."

But Zeus refused to decide. He knew that no matter whom he picked, he would be left with two very angry goddesses.

"Go ask Paris, the prince of Troy," said Zeus. "People say he is the fairest of men, so he should choose the fairest goddess."

The three goddesses found Paris on a mountain. They demanded that he judge them. Each promised him a reward if he chose her.

"Choose me," whispered Hera. "I will give you great power and riches."

Athena said, "Choose me. I will give you great wisdom and victory in every battle you fight."

Then Aphrodite said, in her sweet, warm voice, "Paris, choose me. I will give you the most beautiful woman in the world for your wife."

Paris quickly made up his mind. He gave the apple to Aphrodite.

So Aphrodite cast a spell over Helen, the most beautiful woman in the world. Paris talked her into leaving Greece and sailing to Troy with him.

But there was one big problem. Helen was already married to a Greek king. When the king found out that Paris had taken his wife, he was furious. To get his wife back, he declared war on Troy. He asked the gods to help him.

Paris convinces Helen to follow him to Troy.

The gods took sides. Hera and Athena were still angry with Paris. They chose to fight with the Greeks against Troy. But Aphrodite, to whom Paris had given the golden apple, was on Troy's side.

The Greeks gathered their weapons, boarded their ships, and set sail to attack the great city of Troy. So, with an argument over a golden apple, the Trojan War began.

A Land of City-States

Ancient Greece was not one country with a president or king. Instead, it was a land of **city-states**.

What's a city-state? A city-state is a city and the land around it, with its own army and its own laws. Each Greek city-state had its own ruler.

In some Greek city-states, citizens gathered to discuss their ideas.

The Greek city-states were like brothers and sisters in a family. Sometimes they argued and fought against each other. But like brothers and sisters, the city-states had a lot in common.

Everyone in the city-states spoke the same language, Greek. And they all believed in the same gods and goddesses.

Let's learn more about two very different city-states, Sparta and Athens.

SPARTA: HOME OF THE BRAVE

The people of the city-state called Sparta liked sports and battle. The men of Sparta spent much of their lives preparing for war.

Today, a boy or girl must be almost grown-up to train to fight in a war. But Spartan boys began training for war when they were only seven years old.

When a Spartan boy was seven years old, he left his mother. He went to an army camp to live with soldiers. He learned to run, jump, wrestle, fight, and hunt. He got very little clothing and very little food. If he wanted more to eat, he had to sneak out and hunt wild animals on his own. The Spartans thought this would teach the boy to be strong.

A Spartan soldier bravely carried his shield and weapons into battle.

MAJOR CITY-STATES OF GREECE

Athens and allies

Sparta and allies

0   50   100 km

0   50   100 mi

N
W   E
S

*Black
Sea*

GREECE

Ithaca

Delphi

*Aegean
Sea*

Olympia

Athens

Mycenae

*Ionian
Sea*

Sparta

Mediterranean Sea

When the boys grew up, they became soldiers. They lived to fight. When a Spartan boy left for war, his mother would say, "Come back with your shield or on it." This meant, "Win or die."

The Spartans carried very large shields in battle. A soldier who lost his shield was shamed.

When a Spartan soldier was killed, his body was laid upon his shield and carried home. He was honored for dying bravely.

THE MEANING OF *SPARTAN*

The Spartans lived hard lives. Even today, we call a person "Spartan" who lives a strict life with few comforts.

ATHENS: BIRTHPLACE OF DEMOCRACY

The Spartans prized war, honor, and glory. But the Athenians loved debate, wisdom, and beauty.

In Sparta, you would not find fine buildings or pretty pictures. But the Athenians built beautiful buildings, like the temple called the Parthenon. The artists of Athens carved beautiful statues for their buildings.

In Sparta, men and women were taught to follow orders. But the people of Athens said, "Instead of having one king or just a few rich families in charge, the *people* should help rule the city."

In ancient Athens a very important new idea was born— the idea of **democracy**. *Democracy* means "the people rule."

As part of their democracy, Athenian citizens discussed the best ways to rule their city-state.

19

Beautiful statues
decorate this
Athenian building
built about 420 B.C.

Democracy in Athens was not perfect. It did not include all the people. In Athens, the citizens voted to choose their leaders. But only free adult men were citizens. Women and slaves were not citizens.

Even though democracy in Athens was not perfect, it was still a bold new idea. In most ancient lands, the people were ruled by kings or by the strongest soldiers or by a few rich men. But in Athens, the citizens could finally rule themselves.

This idea of democracy was so important that it has lasted for more than two thousand years. Today, many countries, including the United States, have democratic governments.

FAIRNESS IN GOVERNMENT

In Athens, the citizens gathered in a public meeting called the Assembly. In the Assembly, they discussed many things. Should a law be changed? Should they go to war? Should they choose new leaders? The Athenian citizens talked, argued, and made the decisions for themselves.

Athenians wanted fair government. To prevent rich men from buying votes and power, they cast lots to pick their leaders. Imagine putting names into a hat and drawing some names out. Everyone has an equal chance.

THE ANCIENT WORLD: NO EQUAL RIGHTS

In most of the ancient world, women and slaves did not have the same rights as free adult men. Slaves were common in ancient Greece and other ancient civilizations.

What happened when people committed crimes? Athenians wanted fair decisions, so a **jury** of citizens decided how to punish someone accused of a crime. Sometimes two hundred or more citizens would make up the jury.

The citizens on the jury would use bronze tokens to vote. A token with a solid center meant "innocent." A token with a hole in the middle meant "guilty." Athenians thought it was an honor to serve on a jury.

22

CHAPTER 4

A Day with a Boy in Athens

What was everyday life like in ancient Greece? Let's imagine part of a day in the life of Nestor, an 11-year-old boy in Athens.

This cutaway drawing lets you look inside a home in ancient Athens.

GETTING READY

The morning sun shines through the open windows, waking young Nestor. As his feet touch the damp earth floor of his home, Nestor shivers. He knows it will be hot by afternoon, and the mud-dried bricks of his home will be warm to the touch. But this morning, it is chilly.

He slips on a knee-length **tunic** made of wool. The family raises sheep, and his mother and sisters spin the wool into thread and cloth.

Nestor walks to the well in the open courtyard in the center of his home. As he enters the courtyard, he stops at the family **altar** and says a quick prayer to Athena. Then he draws water from the well. He washes and rubs himself with olive oil.

Nestor enters the common room to have his breakfast. This morning, there are figs, olives, and bread. Nestor dips his bread in olive oil.

"Mother," he says, "is there any meat?"

The Greeks wore loose clothing, like the tunics on these men and women.

"No, Nestor. No one has been hunting."

"We should cook one of our sheep," says Nestor.

"Now, Nestor," his mother replies. "You know we can't kill one of our own animals for food unless we make a special sacrifice. Finish your breakfast and get ready for school."

ANCIENT GREEK SCHOOL SUPPLIES

In ancient Greece, students used a stylus, a kind of a pen. It was made of bone or **bronze**, and had a point on the end. Students wrote by pressing the stylus point on wooden tablets covered with wax.

Students also wrote on **papyrus**, a kind of paper made from the stem of the papyrus plant. It was expensive to make. To write on papyrus, students used pens made from reeds and ink made from soot.

To help with arithmetic, students used a counting board. They moved beads up and down grooves in the board. Each row stood for a different place value, such as tens, hundreds, and thousands.

Above: Counting board

Left: Student with stylus and wooden tablet

Nestor is glad that he is a boy, because only boys go to school. Even though his sisters are learning at home, Nestor likes to go to school. He will be a citizen one day, and he will have the learning he needs to serve his city.

Nestor takes a last bite of bread, and then runs to gather his school things. Today his lessons will be on poetry and public speaking. Yesterday he worked on mathematics. **Philosophy** is his favorite subject. He likes to think and to discuss big questions.

Let's Say It!

- papyrus (puh-PIY-ruhs)
- philosophy (fuh-LAH-suh-fee)

Greek musicians played the lyre, sometimes to provide music to go with songs and poetry.

As he gets ready for school, Nestor hums one of the songs he heard at the symposium his father hosted last night. Nestor enjoys these gatherings. Men from the city come to feast, discuss important topics, recite poetry, and enjoy music. Last night a musician played many songs on a **lyre**.

At these times, Nestor is very glad he is a boy and allowed to visit the symposium. His sisters and mother are not allowed to attend.

IN THE AGORA

On his way to school, Nestor passes through the **agora**, the open-air market in the center of the city. What a busy, noisy place! Fishmongers are selling fish, bakers are selling bread, and farmers are selling fruits, vegetables, and cheeses. Each calls out as Nestor passes.

"Fresh octopus, just off the boats!"

"Come buy my bread—so light and crusty."

"Try this cheese, young master. It is food for the gods!"

Although Nestor has just eaten breakfast, the foods tempt him. As he walks on, the smells of strange spices fill his nose. These spices have come from faraway lands. Nestor knows that merchants leave Athens with pottery, oil, and wool to trade, and he is surprised by what they bring back.

Let's Say It!

- symposium (sim-POH-zee-uhm)
- lyre (liyr)
- agora (A-guh-ruh)

26

In the busy marketplace called the agora, the Greeks came to shop, talk, and have fun.

As Nestor makes his way through the busy agora, he passes craftspeople selling bronze figures, stone carvings, and jewelry. "That necklace would look nice on my sister," he thinks. His sister, Alethia, has just turned 15. This means, as Nestor knows, that she will soon be getting married.

He runs by a group of acrobats and jugglers. He longs to watch, but he knows he must hurry. He doesn't want to be late for school.

Wealthy Greek women could buy gold earrings and other fancy jewelry in the agora.

Nestor squeezes through groups of men who have gathered to talk about the latest news. In his rush, Nestor bumps into a man's leg. He looks up to apologize, but stops in surprise. "Father!"

"In a hurry, my son?" his father smiles. "Off to school with you. Work hard, and grow strong in both mind and body."

As he nears his school, Nestor sees his friend, Darius. They often wrestle each other. Wrestling is part of their training in school. The boys are friends, but when it is time to compete, they both play to win.

"Hello, Darius," says Nestor. "Are you ready to wrestle today?"

"Of course!" says Darius. "I hope you're ready to lose," he says, giving Nestor a playful punch on the shoulder.

"Just be glad you're not wrestling my brother," Nestor replies.

"Will your brother be playing in the games this summer?" asks Darius. "He's a great wrestler. He has a good chance to win."

"Yes," Nestor says with pride. "He will be coming home from the war just for the games."

In school, Greek boys learned wrestling to help keep their bodies fit.

"I wish I had a brother who was a soldier," Darius sighs. "You must be proud that he's fighting the Spartans."

"Oh, I am," says Nestor. "Someday, I will be a soldier, too."

"You?" laughs Darius. "No, Nestor, you won't be a soldier. You will be a philosopher."

"I can be either," Nestor replies. "I have a strong mind *and* a strong body. Just wait till our wrestling match—you'll see!"

THE PELOPONNESIAN WAR

You have learned about two great Greek city-states, Athens and Sparta. These city-states were very different. In 431 B.C., war broke out between them. Some city-states joined the side of the Spartans. Others fought with the Athenians. (See the map on page 18.)

For almost thirty years, the two sides fought each other in what is called the Peloponnesian War. (Greece is a peninsula, sticking out into the sea. The southern part of the peninsula is called the Peloponnese. Sparta and its allies are located there.)

The Athenians had a strong navy. The Spartans had a strong army. Year after year, the two sides battled, but no one could win.

Then a terrible plague struck Athens. Many people fell ill and died. With Athens weakened, the Spartans attacked. By this time the Spartans had built up their own navy. The Spartan fleet defeated the Athenians.

Eventually, Sparta won the war, but all of Greece paid a terrible price. The people had destroyed their farmland and used up their money.

Let's Say It!

• Peloponnesian (peh-luh-puh-NEE-zhuhn)

29

CHAPTER 5

ART AND ARCHITECTURE

The ancient Greeks made beautiful works of art. They built beautiful buildings.

Let's take a closer look at some wonderful examples of what the ancient Greeks made.

The Parthenon, the temple the ancient Greeks built for Athena, still stands today.

The designers of the Lincoln Memorial in Washington, D.C., were inspired by the architects of ancient Greece.

THE PARTHENON

In Athens, there is a high hill called the Acropolis. Today, you can climb this hill and walk around the **ruins** of the Parthenon.

The Parthenon is a shining example of Greek **architecture**. The Greeks built this temple about 2,500 years ago. They built it to honor the goddess Athena.

The Parthenon was made from white marble. Wide, smooth steps led up to it. The temple was more than 60 feet (18 meters) high. Imagine how hard it was to build such a tall building with no modern machines.

This model shows what the Parthenon looked like when it was first built.

Let's Say It!
- Acropolis (uh-KRAH-puh-luhs)
- architecture (AHR-kuh-tek-chur)

All around the Parthenon were columns. The Greeks used columns in many of their buildings. Today, you can still see many buildings made with columns, such as banks and museums.

THREE KINDS OF COLUMNS

On their buildings, the ancient Greeks used three different kinds of columns: Doric, Ionic, and Corinthian.

Doric columns were the simplest. Ionic columns were fancier than Doric. Corinthian columns used complicated designs. Although there are some Greek buildings with Corinthian columns, the design became more popular later during the Roman Empire.

The top of a column is called the *capital*. Some columns have a base, called a *plinth*. Running up and down the sides of a column are grooves called *flutes*.

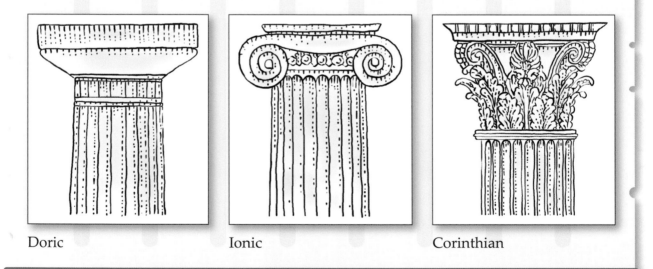

Doric   Ionic   Corinthian

Let's Say It!

- Ionic (iy-AH-nihk)
- Corinthian (kuh-RINT-thee-uhn)

On some buildings, the Greeks carved a long band of designs or pictures, called a **frieze**. Sometimes the pictures in a frieze tell a story. This frieze shows part of a mythical battle between the Greek gods and a fierce band of giants.

LIFELIKE STATUES

Greek **sculptors** paid careful attention to the details of the human body. They made statues that almost seem to live and breathe.

Many of the statues were carved from marble. Some were made of bronze. Some were covered in gold.

Many statues showed the gods and goddesses. But as the Greeks saw them, most of their gods and goddesses looked just like humans. The Greeks put these statues in their temples.

In Athena's temple, the Parthenon, there was a large statue of Athena. It was so big that the head alone was more than six feet tall.

This lifelike bronze statue probably shows Poseidon, god of the sea. His right hand once held a spear.

Let's Say It!

• frieze (freez)

33

POTTERY: BOTH USEFUL AND BEAUTIFUL

Greek potters used clay to make useful things, such as cups, bottles, and big jars to hold olive oil or wine. They turned many of these useful objects into works of art.

The ancient Greeks decorated their pottery with pictures that tell a story. Some of the pictures tell stories about the brave deeds of Greek heroes. Some tell about the gods and goddesses.

The best pottery came from Athens. The red clay of Athens was easy to work with.

First a potter shaped the clay. Then he carved figures in the clay. Then he painted the background with a special liquid. When the pottery was put in the fire to bake, only the background turned black. The red clay figures stood out.

The red figures on this vase tell a story about the Greek hero we know as Hercules.

CHAPTER 6

GOING TO THE THEATER

Crowds are rushing through the streets of ancient Athens. Everyone is pushing in the same direction.

"Hurry!" says one boy to his friend. "I want to get a good seat."

Where are they going? To the theater. What are they going to see? A play.

In ancient Greece, thousands of people crowded into large outdoor theaters to watch plays.

People in ancient Greece loved to watch plays. Some plays told the stories of gods, goddesses, and heroes. Other plays told stories of Greek kings and warriors. Some plays even made fun of the way that people behaved (or misbehaved).

DAYS OF PLAYS

Today, when you go to see a play, you might go in the evening. The show might last about two hours. But in ancient Greece, people went to the theater during the day. Often they stayed all day long, watching one play after another. Many people brought food because they knew they would be staying a long time. Others bought olives, nuts, and figs from vendors around the theater.

During special festivals, almost everyone went to the theater, day after day. On these days, merchants closed their shops. Soldiers stopped fighting. Some prisoners were even let out of the jails. *Everyone* wanted to see the plays.

The ancient Greeks believed that the audience could learn something from watching plays. Sometimes doctors even told sick people to watch plays as a part of their treatment.

DRAMA AND THESPIANS

Drama is our word for storytelling in the form of a play with actors. The word *drama* comes from a Greek word meaning "action."

Actors are sometimes called *thespians.* That word comes from the name of an actor in ancient Greece, Thespis. He was the first winner of a contest held in ancient Athens to see who could perform the best drama.

Let's Say It!

• thespians (THEH-spee-uns)

WHAT THEATERS LOOKED LIKE

In ancient Greece, most large cities had a theater. The biggest theaters could hold as many as 14,000 people.

These outdoor theaters were shaped like a semicircle. The people sat on long rows of stone seats. The rows went up, like the sides of a bowl, so that everyone could see. Modern theaters and stadiums still use this design.

The bowl shape of the theaters also helped people hear. When the actors spoke, their voices were carried up the sides of the bowl-shaped theater. Even people in the back could hear what the actors were saying on the stage.

In the ruins of this ancient Greek theater, rows and rows of seats rise high, like bleachers in modern stadiums.

THE ACTORS AND THE CHORUS

The actors in ancient Greece were all men. They played both male and female parts.

The actors wore big masks. The masks helped the audience know what the character was like. One mask might show a big grin for a happy character. Another might show a broad scowl for a sad or angry character.

In ancient Greece, only a few actors performed in a play. They acted out the main parts. But behind them stood another group of actors, called the chorus.

The chorus members would sing or chant to help tell the story. Sometimes they might speak to one of the main actors. For example, to an actor playing a boastful king, the chorus might say, "Do not be so proud or the gods will punish you!"

Pictures on an ancient vase show actors performing on a stage. They are wearing masks.

TRAGEDIES AND COMEDIES

The playwrights in ancient Greece wrote both sad plays and happy plays.

The sad plays are called **tragedies**. Tragedies told stories about proud kings or about unhappy families. In these plays, the gods would punish people for their bad actions.

Comedies told happy or funny stories. They made fun of people who behaved in foolish or selfish ways. Some comedies even poked fun at the rulers of the city-states.

Even today, the greatest Greek comedies and tragedies are still performed in theaters. Although thousands of years separate us from the ancient Greeks, we can still be thrilled by seeing these stories on stage.

Greek actors wore masks to show emotions. Which mask might be for a tragedy and which for a comedy?

CHAPTER 7

THE OLYMPIC GAMES

Today, some of the greatest athletes from around the world compete in the Olympic Games. They come to run, swim, jump, wrestle, ski, play soccer, and much more. All hope to leave with a medal—bronze, silver, or, for the very best, gold.

In the ancient Olympics, a relay race runner uses his shield to keep his torch lit before handing it to the next runner.

To see these athletes in action, many people travel to the city where the Olympics are being held. Millions of other people around the world watch the games on television.

There is probably no greater sporting event than the Olympics. And where did the Olympics begin? Yes, in ancient Greece.

THE ANCIENT GAMES

The ancient Greeks believed in training both the mind and the body. They held games to celebrate the best athletes.

The Olympic Games were part of a festival to honor Zeus, the king of the gods. The games took place at the foot of Mount Olympus, which the Greeks believed was the home of the gods. That's where the name, *Olympics*, comes from.

This famous statue from ancient Greece shows an athlete throwing a discus.

In the earliest Olympics, athletes competed in only one event, a running race. Later, more events were added.

OLYMPIC EVENTS

As the Olympic Games grew, the Greeks added new contests. There were still foot races. But now there were also chariot races to see who could drive their horses the fastest.

Athletes hurled long spears called javelins. Who could throw the farthest? And who could throw a discus—a flat stone or metal disc—the farthest? Which wrestler was the strongest?

Greek boys learned to wrestle in school, and the best went on to compete in the Olympics.

WHO COMPETED?

In ancient Greece, the honor of competing in the Olympics was not open to everyone. Only young men and boys could compete. They had to be citizens, and they had to be well-trained athletes.

Today, both women and men compete in the Olympic Games. Modern-day Olympic athletes come from all over the world, not just from Greece.

Who could jump the longest? The Greeks gathered to cheer their favorite champions in these and other Olympic events.

One very hard contest was called the *pankration*. The name came from a Greek word meaning "all power." This contest combined boxing and wrestling. There were very few rules. The athletes were allowed to kick and even to pull each other's hair.

The Greeks also created a contest called the *pentathlon*. It was five sports in one. The winner was the athlete who could throw the discus and javelin the farthest. And jump the longest. And run the fastest. And win the wrestling match. Whew!

Let's Say It!

- pankration (pan-KRAY-shun)
- pentathlon (pen-TATH-luhn)

PEACE DURING THE OLYMPICS

In ancient Greece, the Olympics took place every four years. The games were held in the summer. People came from all of the city-states to compete or to watch the athletes.

As you know, the Greek city-states did not always get along. Sometimes they even fought each other. But when it was time for the Olympic Games, the Greeks stopped fighting. For the three months that the games lasted, all wars were set aside.

No weapons were allowed on Olympic grounds. The athletes were able to pass safely through enemy city-states during the Olympics.

CELEBRATING THE WINNERS

Today, winners in the Olympics receive medals of bronze, silver, and gold. But in ancient Greece, Olympic winners were crowned with wreaths made of olive branches. To the Greeks, the olive leaves stood for peace and victory.

When the winners returned home, they were treated like heroes. Some were honored with statues. And many didn't have to pay taxes for the rest of their lives.

The Greeks honored the winners partly because they had proven themselves to be the strongest and fastest athletes. They also honored them because they knew it took great courage and hard work to be an Olympic champion.

This decoration from a vase shows a winner in the ancient Olympics being crowned with a wreath.

CHAPTER 8

GREAT THINKERS

In ancient Greece, especially in Athens, some people were always thinking and talking about big ideas. The Greeks called these people *philosophers*, a word that means "lovers of wisdom."

In ancient Greece, philosophers— "lovers of wisdom"— gathered to discuss big ideas and important questions.

Philosophers asked many questions. "What are human beings like?" they wondered. "How should we behave? Who should be in charge?"

SOCRATES: A MAN OF MANY QUESTIONS

Imagine you are walking along a street in ancient Athens. You see a crowd gathered under the shade of an olive tree. You go closer to see what is happening.

You hear a man's voice. He is a philosopher, and he is asking questions. One man is answering the questions. But every time he answers, the philosopher responds with another question.

This man who asked so many questions was named Socrates. Today we remember him as the first great Greek philosopher.

More than anything else, Socrates wanted the people of Athens to think about the best ways to live their lives. That is why he asked so many questions.

"What is the right way to live?" asked Socrates. "What is most important in life? What is truly good? What is right and what is wrong?"

Socrates wandered the streets of Athens, talking, teaching, and asking questions. His students listened carefully to his words.

The Greek philosopher Socrates led his students to wisdom by asking them many questions.

Let's Say It!

• Socrates (SAHK-ruh-teez)

But some people did not like Socrates. His questions made them uncomfortable. They said he was a dangerous man. They locked him up in prison.

Socrates died in prison. But his words and ideas lived on in the writings of his student, Plato.

PLATO AND THE ACADEMY

Socrates had many students, but the greatest of them all was Plato.

Plato wrote many books. In these books, he described the talks Socrates had with his students. He wrote down many of the questions that Socrates asked.

Plato turned his house into a school called the Academy. At the Academy, people gathered to talk about big questions. Like Socrates, they asked, "How do we live a good life?"

But at Plato's Academy, philosophers also studied science and math. They asked many questions about the world around them. "Where does the sun go when it sets?" they wondered. "How does a seed turn into a plant?"

Plato often thought about how people should be ruled. Should there be a king or a democracy or something in between? Plato came to believe that people should be ruled by a wise king. It would be hard, however, to find a king as wise and thoughtful as Plato.

Let's Say It!

• Plato (PLAY-toh)

46

ARISTOTLE ASKS "WHY?"

One of Plato's favorite students was a young man named Aristotle. Aristotle became a philosopher, too.

He was always asking, "Why?" Why, he asked, are some people brave while others are cowardly? Why do some kinds of government work better than others?

This detail from a famous painting shows Plato (left) and his favorite student, Aristotle (right).

Let's Say It!

- Aristotle (AIR-uh-stah-tl)

In Aristotle's school, students talked about how the world works.

Aristotle seemed to want to know about *everything*. He looked carefully at many kinds of plants and animals. He asked: Why do birds have feathers? Why is water wet? Why do earthquakes happen? He did not always come up with correct answers, but he never stopped asking questions.

Aristotle, like his teacher Plato, also built a school. At his school, teachers and students walked back and forth as they talked about how the world works. They walked so much that people called it "the walking school."

Aristotle learned about anything and everything he could. Like Plato, Aristotle loved to write. He even wrote the first encyclopedia.

Socrates, Plato, and Aristotle were the three greatest philosophers of ancient Greece. Today, people still read and talk about what they wrote. The men have long since passed away but their ideas live on.

HIPPOCRATES: THE FATHER OF MEDICINE

One ancient Greek thinker changed the way that people thought about sickness and healing. His name was Hippocrates.

Before Hippocrates, most people believed that disease was a punishment. They thought that the gods sent disease if a person had done something wrong.

But Hippocrates studied the way the body works. He realized that sickness was not a punishment from the gods but a problem in the body. He studied ways to cure sickness by treating the body of the patient. For this reason, he is sometimes called the father of modern medicine.

Today, some doctors make a promise called the Hippocratic Oath. Like Hippocrates, they promise to do their best to help their patients get well. They also pledge that they will "never do harm to anyone."

Hippocrates, helping a sick man, taught that illness was not a punishment but a problem in the body.

Let's Say It!

• Hippocrates (hip-AHK-ruh-teez)

HOW WE KNOW, WHAT WE OWE

The ruins of ancient Greek cities and buildings still stand, reminding us of the glory of Greece.

Thousands of years have passed since the glorious days of ancient Greece. How do we know about the people of that time?

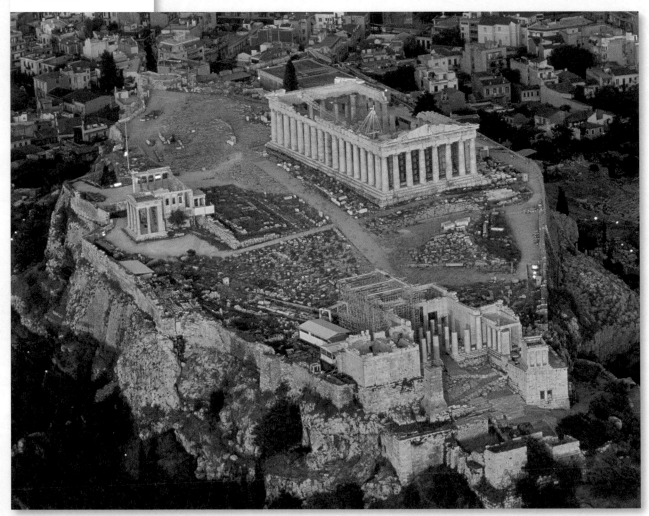

DIGGING UP THE PAST

We know a lot about ancient Greece because of **archaeologists**. Archaeologists are scientists who learn about the past by studying **artifacts** and ruins.

Artifacts are objects that people made and left behind, such as coins, tools, cups, or combs. Archaeologists sometimes find these things when they dig in the ground where people lived long ago. From such artifacts, we can learn about the people who used them and what their lives were like.

Ruins are the remains of the places people built. We know a lot about the Parthenon, for example, because the ruins are still standing today.

Artifacts, like this ancient coin, help us learn about Greece. The owl was a symbol of Athena.

The ruins of this statue lie near the Parthenon. Can you imagine how it once looked?

Let's Say It!

• archaeologists (ahr-kee-AH-luh-jists)

STORIES FROM THE PAST

Another reason we know about ancient Greece is because of the stories that have been passed down for hundreds and hundreds of years. From the stories, we learn about how the ancient Greeks lived and what they believed.

Some of the greatest stories were told by a man called Homer. We don't know much about Homer, but many people think that he was a blind poet. He told tales of brave heroes in great battle, of the gods and goddesses, and of frightening monsters.

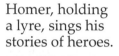

Homer, holding a lyre, sings his stories of heroes.

In Homer's *Odyssey*, Odysseus rescues his crew from the one-eyed monster called the Cyclops.

Year after year, on and on, the Greeks told Homer's stories over and over again. Just about every Greek child grew up hearing tales of the fierce warrior, Achilles, or of the clever hero, Odysseus. We still read Homer's stories today.

SEARCHING FOR ANCIENT GREECE

A little more than 150 years ago, a man in Germany read Homer's stories. His name was Heinrich Schliemann. He loved Homer's stories so much that he read them again and again. Then he thought, "I am going to look for the lands that Homer described in his stories."

Schliemann used the stories to give him clues. He traveled to Greece. He used Homer's words to decide where to dig. In time, he found the sites of ancient cities. He also dug up many valuable artifacts.

Let's Say It!

- Achilles (uh-KIH-leez)
- Odysseus (oh-DIH-see-uhs)
- Heinrich Schliemann (HIYN-rik SHLEE-mahn)

We owe thanks to the ancient Greeks. They gave us much to be thankful for.

They told stories of heroes we still admire. They wrote plays that still thrill us.

They valued art and beauty. They made beautiful statues. They built beautiful buildings. Many modern buildings still use ideas invented by the Greeks.

They believed in strong bodies. They invented the Olympics.

Pericles, a leader of Athens, helped to rebuild the city after a time of war.

Although little remains of the temple of Poseidon, we can imagine its former glory.

They believed in strong minds. They asked important questions. Their great philosophers gave us ideas that still make us think and talk and wonder.

They invented the idea of democracy—the idea that people can rule themselves. Their democracy was not perfect, but it was like a seed that would grow and blossom later.

The time of ancient Greece has long passed, but the glory lives on.

LET'S SAY IT!

At the bottom of some pages in this book, you'll see a symbol followed by words, like this:

• Acropolis (uh-KRAH-puh-luhs)

"Let's Say It!" helps you pronounce some difficult words by respelling those words. The table below lists sample words that explain the sounds of the respellings in this book. For example, *a* represents the short "a" sound in *cat*, while *ay* represents the long "a" sound in *day*. The groups of letters explain how to pronounce more complicated sounds. For example, in the respelling of *Acropolis*—uh-KRAH-puh-luhs—the letters *uh* represent the vowel sound you hear in *shut* and *other*.

VOWELS

a	short a: **a**pple, c**a**t	**iy**	long i: tr**y**, m**igh**t
ay	long a: c**a**ne, d**ay**	**ah**	short o: h**o**t, f**a**ther
e, eh	short e: h**e**n, b**e**d	**oh**	long o: h**o**me, thr**ow**
ee	long e: f**ee**d, t**ea**m	**uh**	short u: sh**u**t, **o**ther
i, ih	short i: l**i**p, act**i**ve	**yoo**	long u: **u**nion, c**u**te

56

LETTER COMBINATIONS

ch	chin, ancient	oo	cool, true, few, rule
sh	show, mission	ow	now, out
zh	vision, azure	ou	look, pull, would
th	thin, health	oy	coin, toy
th	then, heather	aw	saw, maul, fall
ur	bird, further, word	ng	song, finger
us	bus, crust	air	Aristotle, barrister
or	court, formal	ahr	cart, martyr
ehr	error, care		

CONSONANTS

b	butter, baby	n	next, candid
d	dog, cradle	p	price, copper
f	fun, phone	r	rubber, free
g	grade, angle	s	small, circle, hassle
h	hat, ahead	t	ton, pottery
j	judge, gorge	v	vase, vivid
k	kite, car, black	w	wall, away
l	lily, mile	y	yellow, kayak
m	mom, camel	z	zebra, haze

GLOSSARY

agora a marketplace in ancient Greece

altar a table or raised surface used for religious ceremonies

archaeologist a scientist who studies the objects that ancient peoples left behind, such as tools, pottery, buildings, bones, or jewelry

architecture the art of designing buildings

artifacts objects that people made and left behind

bronze a yellow-brown metal made from copper and tin

century a period of 100 years

city-state a city and the land around it, with its own army, laws, and ruler

civilization a culture that has built cities and developed writing, government, and art

comedy a play that tells a happy or funny story, and often pokes fun at human behavior

democracy government by the people

frieze a band of designs or pictures, often carved near the roof or ceiling to decorate a building

jury a group of citizens who meet in a court of law to listen to evidence in order to reach a decision (for example, about whether a person is guilty or innocent)

lyre an ancient stringed instrument, like a small harp

monotheists people who believe in one God

myths imaginative stories that explain events that people once did not understand

papyrus a paper-like material for writing made from the stem of the papyrus plant

peninsula land that has water on all sides but one

philosophy the study of truth, knowledge, and important ideas

polytheists people who believe in many gods

ruins the remaining parts of a building that has been partly destroyed

sculptor an artist who carves a work of art, usually from wood, stone, or metal

tragedy a play that tells a sad story; in ancient Greece, tragedies explored family relationships or relationships between humans and the gods

tunic a long, loose-fitting piece of clothing

ILLUSTRATIONS CREDITS

INDEX